D0788041

The Pelican Chorus
& *The Quangle Wangle's Hat*

EDWARD LEAR
The Pelican Chorus
& *The Quangle Wangle's Hat*

Illustrated by Kevin W. Maddison

A Studio Book

The Viking Press

New York

Illustrations Copyright © 1981 by Kevin W. Maddison

First published in 1981 by The Viking Press (A Studio Book)
625 Madison Avenue, New York, N.Y. 10022

Published simultaneously in Canada by
Penguin Books Canada Limited

Library of Congress Cataloging in Publication Data
Lear, Edward, 1812–1888.
   The pelican chorus and The Quangle Wangle's hat.
   (A Studio book)
   SUMMARY: In two poems the grand King and Queen of the
   Pelicans live a joyous life on the banks of the Nile
   and a strange creature's vast hat attracts a wide
   variety of nesters.
   1. Nonsense-verses, English.   [1. English poetry.
2. Nonsense verses.   3. Pelicans—Poetry]   I. Lear,
Edward, 1812–1888. Quangle Wangle's hat. 1981.
II. Maddison, Kevin W.   III. Title.
PR4879.L2P43 1981   821'.8   80-53511
ISBN 0-670-54613-5

Printed in Japan

The
Pelican Chorus

King and Queen of the Pelicans we;
No other Birds so grand we see!
None but we have feet like fins!
With lovely leathery throats and chins!
Ploffskin, Pluffskin, Pelican jee!
We think no Birds so happy as we!
Plumpskin, Ploshkin, Pelican jill!
We think so then, and we thought so still!

We live on the Nile. The Nile we love.
By night we sleep on the cliffs above;
By day we fish, and at eve we stand
On long bare islands of yellow sand.
And when the sun sinks slowly down
And the great rock walls grow dark and brown,
Where the purple river rolls fast and dim
And the Ivory Ibis starlike skim,
Wing to wing we dance around,—
Stamping our feet with a flumpy sound,—
Opening our mouths as Pelicans ought,
And this is the song we nightly snort;—
    Ploffskin, Pluffskin, Pelican jee,—
    We think no Birds so happy as we!
    Plumpskin, Ploshkin, Pelican jill,—
    We think so then, and we thought so still.

Last year came out our Daughter, Dell;
And all the Birds received her well.
To do her honour, a feast we made
For every bird that can swim or wade.
Herons and Gulls, and Cormorants black,
Cranes, and Flamingoes with scarlet back,
Plovers and Storks, and Geese in clouds,
Swans and Dilberry Ducks in crowds.
Thousands of Birds in wondrous flight!
They ate and drank and danced all night,
And echoing back from the rocks you heard
Multitude-echoes from Bird and Bird,—
    Ploffskin, Pluffskin, Pelican jee,
    We think no Birds so happy as we!
    Plumpskin, Ploshkin, Pelican jill,
    We think so then, and we thought so still!

Yes, they came; and among the rest,
The King of the Cranes all grandly dressed.
Such a lovely tail! Its feathers float
Between the ends of his blue dress-coat;
With pea-green trowsers all so neat,
And a delicate frill to hide his feet, —
(For though no one speaks of it, every one knows,
He has got no webs between his toes!)

As soon as he saw our Daughter Dell,
In violent love that Crane King fell,—
On seeing her waddling form so fair,
With a wreath of shrimps in her short white hair.
And before the end of the next long day,
Our Dell had given her heart away;
For the King of the Cranes had won that heart,
With a Crocodile's egg and a large fish-tart.
She vowed to marry the King of the Cranes,
Leaving the Nile for stranger plains;
And away they flew in a gathering crowd
Of endless birds in a lengthening cloud.
    Ploffskin, Pluffskin, Pelican jee,
    We think no Birds so happy as we!
    Plumpskin, Ploshkin, Pelican jill,
    We think so then, and we thought so still!

And far away in the twilight sky,
We heard them singing a lessening cry,—
Farther and farther till out of sight,
And we stood alone in the silent night!
Often since, in the nights of June,
We sit on the sand and watch the moon;—
She has gone to the great Gromboolian plain,
And we probably never shall meet again!
Oft, in the long still nights of June,
We sit on the rocks and watch the moon;—
   —She dwells by the streams of the Chankly Bore,
And we probably never shall see her more.
      Ploffskin, Pluffskin, Pelican jee,
      We think no Birds so happy as we!
      Plumpskin, Ploshkin, Pelican jill,
      We think so then, and we thought so still!

The
Quangle Wangle's Hat

On the top of the Crumpetty Tree
   The Quangle Wangle sat,
But his face you could not see,
   On account of his Beaver Hat.
For his Hat was a hundred and two feet wide,
With ribbons and bibbons on every side
And bells, and buttons, and loops, and lace,
So that nobody ever could see the face
     Of the Quangle Wangle Quee.

The Quangle Wangle said
    To himself on the Crumpetty Tree,—
'Jam; and jelly; and bread;
    'Are the best food for me!
'But the longer I live on this Crumpetty Tree
'The plainer than ever it seems to me
'That very few people come this way
'And that life on the whole is far from gay!'
    Said the Quangle Wangle Quee.

But there came to the Crumpetty Tree,
    Mr. and Mrs. Canary;
And they said,—'Did you ever see
    'Any spot so charmingly airy?
'May we build a nest on your lovely Hat?
'Mr. Quangle Wangle, grant us that!
'O please let us come and build a nest
'Of whatever material suits you best,
      'Mr. Quangle Wangle Quee!'

And besides, to the Crumpetty Tree
   Came the Stork, the Duck, and the Owl;
The Snail, and the Bumble-Bee,
   The Frog, and the Fimble Fowl;
(The Fimble Fowl, with a Corkscrew leg;)
And all of them said,—We humbly beg,
  'We may build our homes on your lovely Hat,—
  'Mr. Quangle Wangle, grant us that!
     'Mr. Quangle Wangle Quee!'

And the Golden Grouse came there,
   And the Pobble who has no toes,—
And the small Olympian bear,—
   And the Dong with a luminous nose.
And the Blue Baboon, who played the flute,—
And the Orient Calf from the Land of Tute,—
And the Attery Squash, and the Bisky Bat,—
All came and built on the lovely Hat
     Of the Quangle Wangle Quee.

And the Quangle Wangle said
    To himself on the Crumpetty Tree,—
'When all these creatures move
    'What a wonderful noise there'll be!'
And at night by the light of the Mulberry moon
They danced to the Flute of the Blue Baboon,
On the broad green leaves of the Crumpetty Tree,
And all were as happy as happy could be,
        With the Quangle Wangle Quee.